The Children's Nativity

With

Family Devotions
and Activities

Marti McCartney

Illustrated by
Martha Brohammer

Copyright ©2011 Marti McCartney

ISBN
978-0-9764666-7-3

Cover Art and Illustrations by
Martha Brohammer

Text edited by Ann Everett

All rights reserved. No part of this book may be reproduced or transmitted in any form or by any means electronic or mechanical, including photo copying, recording, or by any information storage and retrieval system without written permission from the copyright owner.

Tanos Books
publishing

1110 West 5th Street
Coffeyville, Kansas 67337

Printed in United States of America

Table of Contents

Introduction	Page	5
Foreword		7
Dedication		9
Special Thanks		11
Daily Devotions		13
Instruction Manual		71
Epilogue		87
Appendix A (Epiphany)		89
Appendix B (Date Cake Recipe)		91
Appendix C (Physical Layout)		93
Marti McCartney		95
Alphabetical Index		97
Martha Brohammer		99

Introduction

The Bible is a history book.
History becomes living history when the reader can interact with the written word through personal experiences or memories.

The Children's Nativity is a family devotional from November 28 to December 25, which progressively builds an interactive nativity scene.

Bible verses came from:
Harper Study Bible Revised Standard Version
Harold Lindsell, Ph.D., D.D.
Zondervan Bible Publishers
Grand Rapids, Michigan

Foreword

The Children's Nativity began as my young children interacted with our nativity set by adding dolls and toys to represent the innkeeper, his family and their activities. They wanted to know what he actually did and how he lived. Did he have a dog? Was he married with children? Since there is no documentation in the Bible concerning the innkeeper, inn and stable, we researched Bethlehem as our home school project.

During the time Jesus was born there were reputable innkeepers with families. It was the custom for women to help each other during childbirth, therefore, it is likely the innkeeper's wife or even a mid-wife attended Mary throughout her delivery. Buildings stood alone or were built in an adjacent series surrounding a courtyard or barnyard. Some buildings were found to have the animals on the street level with the household on the second and third levels. Even the roof was used for sleeping or storage.

Each year my children built a different nativity scene using plastic building bricks, wooden interlocking logs, building blocks, rocks, and sticks, as well as, articles around the house. Our family tradition was adding a new figurine to our nativity scene each year. I wrote a daily devotion, story and created an activity for each new addition. These writings became our Advent Devotions, which developed into The Children's Nativity.

Enjoy your family time.
Marti McCartney

Dedication

To my brown-eyed children,
Katherine Elizabeth and Joseph Michael,
who unknowingly provided the vision for this book
with their insatiable curiosity.

In memory of my parents: Dale and Melba Wilcox Rice.

To all who search for meaning, purpose and
value in your lives.

Special Thanks

Special thanks to Ann Everett, my editor, who taught me
dedication and perseverance make ideas reality.

Many thanks to Martha Brohammer, whose illustrations
made it possible for us to see beyond the
simple, written word.

To Taylor Garrett - for making me look good
on the back cover, I thank you.

DAILY DEVOTIONS

November 28

    Once upon a time, a long time ago in Bethlehem, before Jesus was born, lived an innkeeper, his wife and their two children. The innkeeper used good, solid dirt when he built his inn and stable in Bethlehem. The dirt he chose was also good for planting a garden and pastures for his livestock. His children liked to play in the soft, cool dirt.

Devotions – November 28

Addition: Dirt
The inn and stable where Jesus was born had been built on dirt. Dirt represents the Creation of Man. God created man from dirt and gave him life. God created each one of us.

Bible reading: Genesis 2:7
Then the Lord God formed man of dust from the ground, and breathed into his nostrils the breath of life; and man became a living being.

Family Discussion:
What have you made or grown from dirt?

Let us pray:
Lord, We come from dust and to dust we must return. Through you we have a gift of salvation, so we can have everlasting life. Amen.

Activity: Initial set up
Choose, organize and set up the location for your nativity scene. Add dirt and the innkeeper family. See Instruction Manual, page 71.

November 29

    The innkeeper built a sturdy foundation of rocks for his inn and stable. The inn was clean and dry. The stable had stalls for animals and nesting boxes for his chickens. Animals, feed and tools were also kept in the stable. His inn and stable were ready for travelers arriving in Bethlehem for the census.

Devotions - November 29

Addition: Rocks
Rocks represent foundations. Christians should build the foundations of their lives on the Bible.

Bible reading: Matthew 7:24
Everyone then who hears these words of mine and does them will be like the wise man who built [the foundation of] his house upon the rock.

Family Discussion:
How does the Bible build your life's foundation on Jesus?

Let us pray:
Lord, Help us build our lives on you. You are the only foundation we will ever need! Help us not only to hear your words, but also to really believe them. Trusting in you, we walk more serenely each day. Amen.

Activity: Develop nativity site
Build and add inn, stable and stone accessories. Move innkeeper family around each day to show activity. See Instruction Manual, page 71.

November 30

The Innkeeper had a supply of wood for his fires. Wood was used to build the mangers in his stable and the furniture in the inn. He taught his son carpenter skills. The innkeeper and his son built a water trough for the animals. The son constructed his first table and placed it in the inn.

Devotions – November 30

Addition: Wood
Wood represents the wood in the Christian cross. Jesus died for our sins on a wooden cross.

Bible reading: John 19:17,18
So they took Jesus, and He went out, bearing his own cross, to the place called the place of a skull, which is called in Hebrew Golgotha. There they crucified him and with him two others, one on either side, and Jesus between them.

Family Discussion:
How big do you think the cross was?

Let us pray:
Lord, We know we can trust you. Grant that we may always wear your cross in our hearts, admit our sins, and eagerly look to you for the healing we need. Amen

Activity: Add wooden accessories
Build and add manger and wooden accessories. See Instruction Manual, page 71.

December 1

The innkeeper taught his wife and children obedience and respect for God. Every night they studied the word of God and said their prayers. They practiced the Ten Commandments and the customs of their church. They learned a savior would be sent for their salvation. They set their hope in God and His works.

Devotions – December 1

Addition: Joseph
Joseph represents obedience. When the angel told Joseph to take Mary as his wife, he did. Like Joseph we must obey the Word of God.

Bible reading: Matthew 1:20,21 & 24
But as he [Joseph] considered this, behold, an angel of the Lord appeared to him in a dream, saying, "Joseph, son of David, do not fear to take Mary your wife, for that which is conceived in her is of the Holy Spirit, she will bear a son, and you shall call his name Jesus, for He will save his people from their sins." When Joseph woke from sleep, he did as the angel of the Lord commanded him; he took his wife, but knew her not until she had borne a son; and he called his name Jesus.

Family Discussion:
How do you feel when you obey without questioning or arguing?

Let us pray:
Lord, you obeyed the Heavenly Father's will. You were born to die on the cross to take away our sins. Help us to listen to and obey your teachings. Amen

Activity: Obey without arguing
Add Joseph. See instruction Manual, page 71.

December 2

    The Innkeeper was proud of his wife as she humbly served her family and guests with respect and dignity. She prepared delicious, nutritious meals. Her home was clean and comfortable. The Innkeeper's wife prayed for her children every day. She taught them kindness, generosity, and the traditions of their family.

Devotions – December 2

Addition: Mary
Mary represents servitude. Mary models the perfect, humble servant as the mother of Jesus. Christmas invites each one of us to enter into the Lord's service as His servant.

Bible reading: **Luke 1:38**
And Mary said [to the angel, Gabriel] "Behold, I am the handmaid of the Lord; let it be to me according to your word." And the angel departed from her.

Family Discussion:
How are you a servant for the Lord?

Let us pray:
Lord, Your mother was the true example of servitude. Help us to serve others without thought of reward. Make us truly grateful for everyone who serves us because they first loved you. Amen.

Activity: Children plan and make supper.
Add Mary to Joseph. See Instruction Manual, page 71.

December 3

    The innkeeper cleaned and filled his lamps with oil to provide light for his family and guests. His wife made candles for the lanterns that were hung in the stable and inn. The innkeeper and his son used the lanterns when they did chores late at night and early in the morning. At night the campfires of the shepherds were seen on distant hills.

Devotions - December 3

Addition: LIGHT
Light is in the nativity scene because light comes from a flame, which represents prayer. In Bethlehem, where Jesus was born, lamps burned to produce a flame for light. Prayer is the light that will keep our faith burning like the flame of the lamp.

Bible reading: Matthew 5:15, 16
Nor do men light a lamp and put it under a bushel, but on a stand, and it gives light to all in the house. Let your light so shine before men, that they may see your good works and give glory to your Father who is in heaven.

Family Discussion:
Where are places you can pray?

Let us pray:
Lord, You are the light of the world. Shine in our hearts, so that we may let our lights shine for you in all that we do. Help us to understand more fully and enter more wholeheartedly into your plan for our lives. Amen.

Activity: Eat by candlelight.
Move Mary and Joseph closer to the inn. Add light representations. See Instruction Manual, page 71.

December 4

The innkeeper dug a deep well that has good, cool, fresh, clean water. The innkeeper's son keeps the water troughs in the stable filled with clean water for the animals. His daughter fills the water jugs that are kept in the inn for the family and guests. They use water for cooking and to keep clean. The washstand is just inside the door of the inn.

Devotions - December 4

Addition: WATER
Water represents baptism. The water of Baptism washes away our sins, so we may have the gift of eternal life with our loving Savior.

Bible reading: Acts 2:38
And Peter said to them, [the apostles] "Repent and be baptized every one of you in the name of Jesus Christ for the forgiveness of your sins, and you shall receive the gift of the Holy Spirit."

Family Discussion:
What do you need to do to be baptized?

Let us pray:
Lord, Your blessings flow like water, abundantly, and in so many ways. Thank you for refreshing and cleansing us. Do not let our lack of faith or hope lesson your power to work through us. Amen.

Activity: Drink water with supper.
Move Mary and Joseph closer to the inn. Add water and containers. See Instruction Manual, page 71.

December 5

    The Innkeeper has been working in the stable cleaning the stalls and adding fresh straw. Some of his guests that are coming to Bethlehem for the census will need a place for their animals to stay. He also put a large stack of straw in the corner for them to use. The stable now has the smell of clean, fresh straw.

Devotions - December 5

Addition: STRAW
Straw represents preparation. During these weeks proceeding Christmas we are preparing ourselves to live as Christians.

Bible reading: **Matthew 24:44**
Therefore you also must be ready; [prepared] for the Son of man is coming at an hour you do not expect.

Family Discussion:
How are you preparing your life to live as a Christian?

Let us pray:
Lord, You traveled all the way to Earth to be our Savior. Help us prepare our lives for your coming. May the way we live, and the way we are to others, be an effective proclamation to your presence in our lives. Amen.

Activity: Make straw accessories.
Move Mary and Joseph closer to the inn. Add straw. See Instruction Manual, page 71.

December 6

    The innkeeper has a supply of grain in the stable. He used the grain for seed for planting and feed for his animals. When the grain is ripe they harvest it for storage. His wife cooks some of the grain for the family to eat. The innkeeper and his son take some of the wheat to the miller to be ground into flour. His chickens like to eat cracked corn.

Devotions – December 6

Addition: GRAIN
Grain represents growth. We must plant the word of God in our hearts in order to grow in our walk as a Christian.

Bible reading: Matthew 13:31-32
Another parable He [Jesus] put before them, saying, "The kingdom of heaven is like the grain of a mustard seed, which a man took and sowed in his fields; it is the smallest of all seeds, but when it has grown it is the greatest of shrubs and becomes a tree, so that the birds of the air come and make nests in its branches."

Family Discussion:
What have you grown from a seed?

Let us pray:
Lord, Thank you for your very precious promise of salvation and for all you do to make it come true for us. Help us to trust your work with faith like that of a mustard seed. Amen.

Activity: Bake oatmeal cookies.
Move Mary and Joseph closer to the inn. Add grains.

December 7

      The innkeeper has two oxen that are yoked together to pull his wagon and plow. His children are careful around the oxen. The oxen are used to tread* out the grain that is taken to the miller for grinding. His wife makes shoes for the family from the hide. His daughter makes spoons from the horns.

*The oxen are tied to a post so they walk round and round in a circle over the stalks of grain causing the grain to separate from the hulls (chaff) and dried plants.

Devotions – December 7

Addition: OXEN
Oxen represent gifts from God. The oxen give us food and clothing. Its horns can even be made into instruments or used as tools. The oxen also make good draft animals.

Bible reading: Genesis 1:28
God blessed man and said, "Be fruitful and increase in number; fill the Earth and subdue it. You are to rule over the fish of the sea, the birds of the air and over every living creature that moves on the ground: And God said, "I give you every seed-bearing plant on the face of the Earth and every tree that has fruit with seed in it. They will be yours for food."

Family Discussion:
What have you created as a gift for someone?

Let us pray:
Lord, Some of the things you provide for us are so basic that we don't even remember to say, "Thank you." Help us to remember the gifts we have received and share them with our friends and family. Amen.

Activity: Eat beef and dairy products for supper.
Move Mary and Joseph closer to the inn. Add oxen.

December 8

    The Innkeeper's wife keeps a mousetrap next to the kitchen stove. There are also cats in the stable to chase away the mice from the grain. The Innkeeper's daughter's favorite cat is the small white one. It likes to chase her weaving yarn. Her mother told her the cat should stay outside and not be in the house.

Devotions – December 8

Addition: MOUSETRAP
Mousetrap represents sin. Sin is always present. It is easy to get caught in the trap of thinking something we are doing wrong could be the right thing to do.

Bible reading: Psalms 1:1
Blessed is the man who walks not in the counsel of the wicked, nor stands in the way of sinners, nor sits in the seat of scoffers; but his delight is in the law of the Lord, and on his law he meditates day and night.

Family Discussion:
What do you consider to be a sin?

Let us pray:
Lord, Our hearts grieve and we are sorry when we do not listen to your teaching and sin against you. Please deliver us from evil and forgive us of our sins. Amen.

Activity: Eat fruit or vegetables in Jell-O.
Move Mary and Joseph closer to the inn. Add mousetrap.

December 9

The innkeeper has a faithful, hard working dog that protects the innkeeper and his family. The dog sleeps in the inn and barks when someone knocks on the door or when it thunders. The innkeeper's son takes the dog with him when he herds the sheep. There are new puppies in the stable.

Devotions – December 9

Addition: DOG
Dogs represent faithfulness. A dog is faithful to a good and caring master. Our master is the Lord. He is so faithful that He laid down his life for us.

Bible reading: **Romans 8:38-39**
For I am sure that neither death, nor life, nor angels, nor principalities, nor things present, nor things to come, nor powers, nor height, nor depth, nor anything else in all creation, will be able to separate us from the love of God in Christ Jesus our Lord.

Family Discussion:
How do you know when someone is faithful to you?

Let us pray:
Lord, We know that you care for us and you are always faithful and will never leave us. We will pray to you, worship you, and study your word faithfully as long as we live.   Amen.

Activity: Write and send a letter.
Move Mary and Joseph closer to the inn. Add dog.

December 10

    The innkeeper's wife and daughter make the bread for the family and guests at the Inn. It smells so good when the bread is baking. The innkeeper's son likes to eat the bread when it is hot from the oven. They always bake an extra loaf for the widow next door. Sometimes they make fried bread by rolling the dough very thin and frying it in a skillet on top of the stove.

Devotions – December 10

Addition: BREAD
Bread represents communion. When we take Holy Communion we remember that Christ died for our sins. Jesus gave His life for the forgiveness of our sins.

Bible reading: Corinthians 11:23-24
For I [Paul] received from the Lord what I also delivered to you, that the Lord Jesus on the night when He was betrayed took bread, and when He had given thanks, He broke it, and said, "This is my body which is for you. Do this in remembrance of me."

Family Discussion:
How does your family take communion?

Let us pray:
Lord, You provide so much, so much more than we could ever even ask for. Help us to receive our daily bread with thanksgiving. May your word fill us, nourish us and give us the love to share what we receive from you with others. Amen

Activity: Bake bread.
Move Mary and Joseph closer to the inn. Add bread.

December 11

One day when the innkeeper and his family were eating, one of his goats stood up on his hind legs to look through the kitchen window, which made everyone laugh. The innkeeper has a small herd of goats. They make cheese from the goat's milk. The innkeeper's son likes his mother's goat stew.

Devotions – December 11

Addition: GOAT
Goats represent laughter. The goat may be the funniest of all animals in the stable as he bounces around getting into mischief. People get into mischief too, which can be frustrating, but if we look, we can see the good in people as well and laugh with them, too.

Bible reading: **Psalms 133:1**
Behold, how good and pleasant it is when brothers and sisters dwell in unity!

Family Discussion:
How do you feel when you laugh with your friends and family?

Let us pray:
Lord, Thank you for everything that makes us laugh. Please help us look for the laughter in people. Thank you for promising us a heavenly home filled with even more joy and laughter. Amen.

Activity: Tell a funny family story.
Move Mary and Joseph closer to the inn. Add goat.

December 12

Flies pester the animals in the innkeeper's stable, so he keeps narrow necked jugs sitting around the stable and inn. The jugs contain a mixture of vinegar and honey. The flies are attracted to the sweet smell and crawl down the neck of the bottle to get to the liquid, but cannot escape back up the neck of the bottle.

Devotions – December 12

Addition: FLIES
Flies represent unpleasant things. Animals were in the stable. Where there are animals there are flies. Flies are not very pleasant to us, but even unpleasant things have a purpose in God's creation.

Bible reading: Exodus 20:11
For in six days the Lord made heaven and Earth, the sea, and all that is in them, and rested the seventh day; therefore the Lord blessed the Sabbath day and hallowed it.

Family Discussion:
What is something in your life that is unpleasant, but has a purpose?

Let us pray:
Lord, You suffered for us in many ways. By your suffering our sins are taken away. Thank you for every unpleasant thing you did for us. Amen.

Activity: Sort and gift clothes.
Move Mary and Joseph closer to the inn. Add flies.

December 13

    The innkeeper's wife and daughter weave yarn into beautiful patterns in their blankets. They keep the blankets neat and clean for the family and guests. His daughter is making a blanket to take with her when she is married. His son rolls a blanket into a bedroll to take with him when he tends the sheep at night. The Innkeeper's wife trades her blankets for things she needs from the market.

Devotions – December 13

Addition: BLANKET
Blankets represent security. Animals use fur or feathers for protection. We need the covering and security of the Lord's love to protect not only our soul, but our body as well.

Bible reading: Psalms 94:16-19
Who rises up for me against the wicked? Who stands up for us against evildoers? If the Lord had not been our help, my soul would soon have dwelt in the land of silence. When I thought, "My foot slips," thy steadfast love, O Lord, held me up, when the cares of my heart are many, thy consolations cheer my soul.

Family Discussion:
What does the security of God's love feel like to you?

Let us pray:
Lord, Your forgiveness covers us and makes us pure and clean. Thank you for watching over us and covering us in your protecting love. Amen.

Activity: Sew a quilt block
Move Mary and Joseph closer to the inn. Add blankets.

December 14

    The innkeeper and his family all work with different tools in their gardens, pastures, fields, inn and stable. The innkeeper is teaching his son to use the tools he will need to become an innkeeper and carpenter. His wife is teaching their daughter to use the tools she will need to become a homemaker and mother.

Devotions - December 14

Addition: TOOLS
Tools represent work. A hoe is a tool that is used for working the ground preparing it for seeds or removing weeds. We have work to do as Christians.

Bible reading: Thessalonians 4:11
Aspire to live quietly, to mind your own affairs, and to work with your hands, as we are charged, so that you may command the respect of outsiders, and be dependent on nobody.

Family Discussion:
What tools do you think were used in the inn or the stable?

Let us pray:
Lord, Open our ears to truly hear, open our hands to honestly work, and open our eyes to clearly see each day as a labor of love, done for the glory of you. Amen.

Activity: Bake cutout cookies.
Move Mary and Joseph closer to the inn. Add tools.

December 15

The innkeeper and his family all work the wheat after it has been cut and dried. After the oxen have tread out the grain, the chaff is removed by using a winnowing fork or winnowing basket. When the grain is tossed in the air the wind blows the chaff away and the good grains are then saved for the family to use.

Devotions - December 15

Addition: WINNOWING FORK
A winnowing fork represents forgiveness. A winnowing fork is used to separate the grains of wheat from the chaff. The winnowing fork reminds us that Jesus removes our sin from us so that what remains in our lives will be good to use for His service.

Bible reading: Ephesians 4:31
Let all bitterness and wrath and anger and clamor and slander be put away from you, with all malice, and be kind to one another, tenderhearted, forgiving one another, as God in Christ forgave you.

Family Discussion:
How do you forgive someone?

Let us pray:
Lord, Thank you for thinking that I am worth keeping! Thank you for all you did to make me yours! Thank you for the wonder of my being! Amen.

Activity: Drink tea.
Move Mary and Joseph closer to the inn. Add winnowing fork.

December 16

    The innkeeper has a flock of chickens. Everyday the children take grain and water to the chickens. The children also gather the eggs for their mother to use for cooking. The chickens eat the bugs that get in the garden. The rooster crows very early in the morning, which the son does not like.

Devotions - December 16

Addition: EGGS
Eggs represent salvation. An egg carries the hope of a new life. Our salvation is our new life.

Bible reading: Psalms 68:19-20
Blessed be the Lord, who daily bears us up; God is our salvation. Our God is a God of salvation; and to God, the Lord, belongs our escape from death.

Family Discussion:
What is salvation like for you?

Let us pray:
Lord, Let us not be ashamed of our faith in you and our salvation. Let our new lives show others the love you have for us. Let us show our love for you to others. Amen.

Activity: Eat eggs.
Move Mary and Joseph closer to the inn. Add eggs.

December 17

    The innkeeper made a new rope and put it on the bucket for his well. When he was a little boy, his father taught him how to make good, strong ropes using three stands of hemp. He then taught his son how to make the good ropes and showed him how to make a rope halter for the oxen.

Devotions - December 17

Addition: ROPE
Rope represents friendship. A rope can be used to tie things together. We need to tie our relationships and trust to other Christians.

Bible reading: Ecclesiastes 4:9, 10
Two [people] are better than one, because they have a good reward for their toil. For if they fall, one will lift up his fellow; but woe to him who is alone when he falls and has not a friend to lift him up.

Family Discussion:
What things do you do to show your friends you care about them?

Let us pray:
Lord, You are our friend. You reached out to rescue us, and now we are tied to you in friendship. We know you will never let us go! We want to know you. We want to do your will. We trust that you will make your way clear to us. Amen.

Activity: Invite friends over.
Move Mary and Joseph closer to the inn. Add rope.

December 18

When the innkeeper travels he uses a two-wheeled cart. He also has a wheel in the stable that he is repairing. Making a good round wheel is hard work. His friend is a wheelwright. When his friend stays in the inn he pays for his room by making new wheels for the innkeeper.

Devotions - December 18

Addition: WHEEL
Wheels represent eternity. Wheels help us travel. It is good to visit, but it is good to come home, too. The journey of a Christian life will bring us to our eternal home in heaven.

Bible reading: Psalm 73:23, 24
Nevertheless I am continually with thee [the Lord]; thou dost guide me with thy counsel, and afterward thou wilt receive me to glory.

Family Discussion:
What are you doing to prepare for your home in heaven?

Let us pray:
Lord, Welcome to our home! Because of your love for us we know we will feel welcome when you come for us to live with you in our eternal heavenly home.   Amen

Activity: Eat doughnuts.
Move Mary and Joseph closer to the inn. Add wheels.

December 19

    The innkeeper's son is the shepherd for his father's flock of sheep. He keeps the sheep safe when he goes to the pastures in the hills by keeping them together. The family dog goes with him to help guard the sheep. Sometimes he must spend the night, so he takes his bedroll and a bag his mother packed with bread, cheese, olives, dates, rice and a bottle of milk.

Devotions - December 19

Addition: SHEPHERDS
Shepherds represent caring. Shepherds were the first to be told the good news that our Savior had been born. Jesus is our shepherd.

Bible reading: Psalm 23
The lord is my shepherd, I shall not want; He makes me lie down in green pastures. He leads me beside still waters; He restores my soul. He leads me in the paths of righteousness for His name's sake. Even though I walk through the valley of the shadow of death, I fear no evil; for Thou are with me; Thy rod and Thy staff, they comfort me. Thou preparest a table before me in the presence of my enemies; thou anointest my head with oil, my cup overflows. Surely goodness and mercy shall follow me all the days of my life; and I shall dwell in the house of the Lord forever.

Family Discussion:
How have your parents lead and guided you?

Let us pray:
Lord, We need you to lead us and guide us, to protect us and care for us, and to bring us safely home to you. Amen.

Activity: Eat a shepherd's meal.
Move Mary and Joseph closer to the inn. Add shepherds.

December 20

The innkeeper uses his flock of sheep for clothing and food. His wife and daughter spin the wool into yarn. They color the yarn red with beet juice, yellow with onionskins, blue with cabbage leaves and green with spinach leaves. They weave the beautifully colored yarn into rugs or cloth to make clothes for the family.

Devotions – December 20

Addition: LAMBS
Lambs represent sacrifice. Sweet and gentle, pure and innocent, the lamb was the perfect sacrifice; the way God would like us to be. Jesus was the Lamb of God.

Bible reading: John 1:29
The next day he [John the Baptist] saw Jesus coming toward him, and said, "Behold, the Lamb of God, who takes away the sin of the world!"

Family Discussion:
What have you sacrificed for Jesus?

Let us pray:
Lord, Take away our sins as we confess them to you and to those that we have sinned against. Have mercy on us, and grant us peace, so we may learn from our mistakes. Amen.

Activity: Make a gift.
Move Mary and Joseph closer to the inn. Add lambs.

December 21

Doves like to eat the grain the innkeeper spills when he feeds his animals, so they built their nests in the trees next to the stable. The innkeeper's children like to watch the graceful birds fly. They make sure the dove's nests are not disturbed. They have fun collecting the beautiful white feathers.

Devotions – December 21

Addition: DOVES
Doves represent peace. The dove is a symbol of peace, an indication that everything is the way it is supposed to be. Jesus gives us peace when we go to Him.

Bible reading: John 14:27
Peace I [Jesus] leave with you; my peace I give to you; not as the world gives do I give to you. Let not your hearts be troubled, neither let them be afraid.

Family Discussion:
What can you do to give peace to someone?

Let us pray:
Lord, Send your Holy Spirit to us. Open our hearts to feel the peace that comes with our acceptance of the Holy Spirit. Amen.

Activity: Bless each other.
"Peace be with you (name) and with this house."
"And with you also."
Move Mary and Joseph closer to the inn. Add doves.

December 22

A large, old, owl lives in the rafters of the innkeeper's stable. She flies out at night to hunt for rodents. The hooting of the owl at night lets the family know the owl is at work protecting their stored grain from the mice. Since the owl flies silently, the children never hear the owl when she leaves or returns.

Devotions – December 22

Addition: OWL
Owls represent wisdom. The owl sits with his eyes looking and ears listening. We are to be attentive like the owl. We are to keep our eyes straightforward, focused on Jesus, so we may learn wisdom and understanding from our Christian instructors as we study the Bible.

Bible reading: Proverbs 1:2, 3
[Study the Bible] That men may learn wisdom and instruction, understand words of insight, receive instruction in wise dealing, righteousness, justice and equity.

Family Discussion:
What do you do in order to make a wise decision?

Let us pray:
Lord, Teach us to hear our father's instruction and learn from our mother's teachings. Let us keep what we have learned about you in our hearts forever. Amen.

Activity: Write a Bible verse on a scroll to memorize.
Move Mary and Joseph closer to the inn. Add Owl.

December 23

The innkeeper and his wife own a donkey. The donkey carries their supplies to and from the market. His wife made baskets that go on both sides of the donkey's back. The donkey is strong, so he can pull a cart for the family. Some of the innkeeper's guests pay him to use the donkey to carry their things.

Devotions - December 23

Addition: DONKEY
Donkeys represent humility. Donkeys are humble animals. Their main job is to carry things for people. We are to walk humbly with the Lord as we carry His word.

Bible reading: **Romans 12:3**
For by the grace given to me I [Paul] bid every one among you not to think of himself more highly than he ought to think, but to think with sober judgment, each according to the measure of faith, which God has assigned him.

Family Discussion:
How do you use your gifts to carry the word of God?

Let us pray:
Lord, You were not ashamed to come as a humble baby for us. Even if people make fun of us, help us never to be ashamed of you or ourselves. Amen.

Activity: Do someone a favor.
Move Mary and Joseph quite near the inn. Add donkey.

December 24

The inn is already filled with families when Joseph desperately knocks on the door. Joseph told the innkeeper that his wife, Mary, was soon to be delivered of her first baby. Quickly the innkeeper's wife and daughter take care of Mary. They prepare a place for her on the clean straw in their stable. They stay with her to help during the delivery of her baby.

Devotions – December 24

Addition: SWADDLING CLOTHES
Swaddling clothes represent love. Mary brought swaddling clothes, so her baby would be warm and clean when He was born. She wanted her baby to feel loved and welcomed into her life. The birth of Jesus assures us that God wraps us in his love.

Bible reading: **John 3:16**
For God so loved the World that He gave His only son, that whoever believes in Him, should not perish but have eternal life.

Family Discussion:
How does God show his love to you?

Let us pray:
Lord, Thank you for the love that holds us close to you. Help us to love others the way you love us. With all our heart we ask you to purify us and prepare us to receive you in our lives this Christmas.   Amen.

Activity: Write appreciation notes to each other.
Move Mary and Joseph so they are talking to the innkeeper. Add swaddling clothes.
Tonight: Add Baby Jesus, angel, star, and wise men.

December 25

    The innkeeper's wife and daughter are pleased; Mary delivered a healthy, baby boy. The innkeeper's wife handed the baby to Mary who wrapped him in the swaddling clothes, nursed him, and laid him in a manger to sleep. Mary and Joseph are thankful for the kindness of strangers.

Devotions – December 25

Addition: BABY JESUS
Jesus represents the fulfillment of God's blessings on us. God has blessed all of us with an eternal life in heaven through the birth of his son, Christ the Lord.

Bible reading: Luke 8
When the shepherds were in the field, watching over their flocks by night. An angel of the Lord appeared to them, and the glory of the Lord shone around them, and they were filled with fear. The angel said to them, "Be not afraid; for behold, I bring you good news of great joy, which will come to all the people, for to you is born this day in the city of David a Savior, who is Christ the Lord."

Family Discussion:
How does it feel to have Jesus in your life?

Bless your family:
Numbers 6, 24-26.
"The Lord bless you and keep you. The Lord makes his face to shine upon you, and be gracious to you. The Lord lifts up his countenance upon you, and gives you peace."
2 Corinthians 13:14.
"The grace of the Lord Jesus Christ and the Love of God and the fellowship of the Holy Spirit, be with you all!"
Amen

Activity: Bake Jesus a birthday cake.
Enjoy the blessings of Christmas.

INSTRUCTION MANUAL

Construction, Additions and Activities

This is an interactive nativity scene. It begins with constructing the inn and stable. Each subsequent day adds items to the nativity scene, which includes the Christian symbolism lessons, a daily devotion and activity.

Additional accessories or figurines can be included on any day. The nativity scene can be as detailed as a landscaped town or as simple as the basic, generic nativity stable. Move pieces around to show activity.

Figurines and accessories

Use commercial figurines, dolls, toys, pictures, drawings, miniatures, or handcrafted sculptures. Card stock drawings folded into an A or L will stand. Nativity figurines and accessories are available through hobby and craft stores or collector sets, such as the Fontanini® Nativity Collection.

NOVEMBER 28

Addition: DIRT
Dirt can be real dirt, sand, an artificial mat, a drape, sheet or just the tabletop or floor. (When I used real dirt, my young children had entirely too much fun playing in it.) Remember, the scene is interactive and little people have a tendency to jostle the scene and tug against table coverings.

Activity: Initial set-up.
Choose and organize the location for your nativity scene. Add dirt and innkeeper family.

Note:
Your current nativity display may be a meaningful part of your Christmas tradition and used for these readings.

Organization tip:
Inventory and date a zip lock bag for each day. The bags are kept together in a plastic, lidded tub.

NOVEMBER 29

Addition: ROCKS
Rocks and pebbles can be used for buildings, boulders, landscaping, bridges, fire pits, steps, fences, roads, wells and ovens. (Burnt match heads make great coals for a fire pit or oven.) Rocks can be glued together and saved for future nativity scenes.

Activity: Build and add the inn and stable.
Optional building materials are plastic building bricks, wooden interlocking logs, building blocks or shoeboxes covered with rock or plank printed scrap-booking pages. Have the children design the buildings and the layout. Add roofs or use half-walls. Build a one or multi-level inn. Look in from the sides or down from the top. It can be different every year. (Refer to Appendix C, page 93.)

NOVEMBER 30

Addition: WOOD
Wooden accessories are used inside and outside the inn, as well as the stable, like barrels, trunks, furniture, dishes, buckets, cabinets, shelves, trunks, tools, crates, wagons, feed troughs (manger), animal yokes, wagons, boards, boxes, benches, stools, fire pits, fences, trees and log piles.
Activity: Build and add manger and wooden items.
Popsicle sticks, wooden interlocking logs and sticks from the yard can be used for the construction of buildings, furniture or the manger. Break twigs to use for fire logs. Twigs stuck in clay can be fences, trees, and bushes. Constructed items can be glued and saved.

DECEMBER 1

Addition: JOSEPH
Joseph can be a figurine, doll, picture, or drawing. He is preparing to leave Nazareth. Place him in another section of the room or house to begin his journey to Bethlehem. He and Mary will be moved closer to the inn each day.
Activity: Obey without arguing.

DECEMBER 2

Addition: MARY
Mary is put with Joseph for their journey. The Fontanini® Nativity Collection has a pregnant Mary on a donkey. Joseph and Mary are now making their journey to Bethlehem for the census. Each day move them a little closer to the inn and stable, in order for them to arrive at the inn and are talking to the innkeeper when the children go to bed on Christmas Eve.
Activity: Children plan and make supper.

DECEMBER 3

Addition: LIGHT
Oil lamps, torches, lanterns, candles and fire pits produce light.
Activity: Eat by candlelight.
Make and add light producing items. Paint the end of sticks red and stick them in clay for torches. Lamps can be sculpted.

DECEMBER 4

Addition: WATER
Water containers are wells, ponds, pitchers, jugs, vases, pottery, mugs, buckets and animal water troughs. Build a pond by adding a mirror surrounded by pebbles or sand and rocks. Stick tiny artificial or dry flowers in sand or clay for plants.
Activity: Drink water with supper.
Make and add water containers.
Note: The foot washing ceremony works well here. See John, Chapter 13.

DECEMBER 5

Addition: STRAW
Grass clippings, floral or model railroading grass can be made into haystacks, straw for the mangers, piles of hay for the animals to eat, sheaves of grass, and nests for fowl.
Activity: Gather grass and make straw accessories.
Hold a handful of grass in a small bunch and tie a string around it for the sheaves. Grass can be snipped into pieces to cover the floor of the stable. Sprinkle grass onto a pile of glue and shape into nests that can be saved.

DECEMBER 6

Addition: GRAIN
Mustard seeds, different flours, cornmeal, salt, pepper, herbs, and spices can be grains. Piles of grain can be in the inn or stable's storage areas or put in pottery or baskets.
Activity: Bake oatmeal cookies.
Use a favorite family recipe, a box mix or frozen cookies.

DECEMBER 7

Addition: OXEN
Activity: Eat beef and dairy products for supper.
Oxen can be figurines, cattle from toy farm sets or drawings on card stock. The card stock can be folded into a 'A' or 'L' in order to stand.

DECEMBER 8

Addition: MOUSETRAP
Traps can be hunter's traps, insect nets, boxes propped up with sticks, fishing poles or cats. A piece of paper or paper clip can be folded to look like a mousetrap. Consider using a picture of your cat.
Activity: Eat fruit or vegetables in Jell-o.
The food trapped in the Jell-o can be seen.

DECEMBER 9

Addition: DOG
Consider using a picture of your dog.
Activity: Write and mail a letter.
Non-writers can draw pictures that have adult captions.

DECEMBER 10

Addition: BREAD
Broken crackers look like flat bread or sculpt clay into bread shapes.
Activity: Bake bread or biscuits.
Bread can be homemade or frozen. Canned biscuits are available.

DECEMBER 11

Addition: GOAT
Activity: Telling Stories
Have each person tell a funny, "remember-when" family story. Make sure these stories are indeed funny and never mocking anyone. Adults tell funny stories from your childhood.

DECEMBER 12

Addition: FLIES
Sprinkled poppy seeds look like flies. Unpleasant animals might be skunks or raccoons. Bees also work.
Activity: Sort and gift clothes
Sort your clothes and gift someone or someplace with the clothes that no longer fit or are no longer worn.

DECEMBER 13

Addition: BLANKET
Pieces of material can be cut or folded into mats, tied into bedrolls, or used for blankets for people or animals.
Activity: Quilt block
Each person makes a quilt block that over the years can collectively be made into a quilt. Remember to date and sign each block with embroidery or permanent ink. A simple quilt block is four equal squares sewn together with ¼" seams to form a larger square. They can be sewn by hand or machine. Perhaps the adults could make the blocks and the children embroidery or draw on the blocks.

DECEMBER 14

Addition: TOOLS
Any kind or size of indoor or outdoor tool will do. Use real tools or miniatures. Consider using drawings, or photographs of your family working and using tools.
Activity: Bake cut out cookies.
Cookies can be a favorite family recipe, frozen or a boxed mix. Talk about all the different tools you are using as you cook.

DECEMBER 15

Addition: WINNOWING FORK
A winnowing fork can be represented with a twig that has several small branches, a kitchen fork or a pitchfork from a toy farm set.
Activity: Steep and drink loose-leaf tea.
When loose-leaf tea is steeped and strained it leaves the good tasting tea to drink, and the tealeaves are then discarded.

DECEMBER 16

Addition: EGGS
Clay or artificial eggs can be put in nests that have been made from grass clippings or put in baskets. Fowl can be added like chickens, ducks, turkeys, birds or geese that can be put in nests, ponds, perched on fences, trees and bushes or they can be eating spilled grain.
Activity: Eat eggs, which can be cooked in a variety of ways like deviled, scrambled or sandwiches.

DECEMBER 17

Addition: ROPE
Yarn, string, or crochet thread can be coiled and tied to look like a rope.
Activity: Invite friends over.
Include your friends in your nativity activities and devotions.

DECEMBER 18

Addition: WHEEL
Any wheel will do even if it is attached to something. Point out all the things around your house with wheels.
Activity: Eat doughnuts.

DECEMBER 19

Addition: SHEPHERD
More than one shepherd can be used. Consider using a picture of the father, grandfathers, uncles or boys in your family for the shepherds.
Activity: Eat the shepherd's meal.
Eat a meal like the innkeeper's wife fixed for her son when he spent the night in the field with the sheep.

DECEMBER 20

Addition: LAMB
Add sheep and lambs. Gluing cotton balls together makes kneeling sheep.
Activity: Make a gift.
Have everyone make a gift or make a family gift. The gift is for someone not living with you.

DECEMBER 21

Addition: DOVES
Fold paper into a V for a dove. Doves can be perching or tied with thread to hang from trees.
Activity: Blessing
Bless each person present (including the reader). Consider blessing absent or deceased family members.

DECEMBER 22

Addition: OWL
Activity: Write a Bible verse on a scroll to memorize.
The innkeeper taught his family about God from scrolls. Scrolls are made with paper rolled into a tube and tied with string. Write from top to bottom, then unroll and re-roll as you read. My children also wanted a miniature Bible in our inn. Not historically correct, but this is your nativity scene so develop it to meet the needs of your family.

DECEMBER 23

Addition: DONKEY
Activity: Do someone a favor.
Note: Remember, Mary and Joseph should be quite near the inn.

DECEMBER 24

Addition: SWADDLING CLOTHES
Swaddling clothes are used to wrap babies securely. You can wrap up the baby or make a cloth bag (like a tiny pillowcase) to use as swaddling clothes.
Activity: Appreciation notes.
Give each family member a note about how special they are in your life. Move Mary and Joseph so they are talking to the innkeeper.
Note: After bedtime add Baby Jesus to the swaddling clothes/bag. Put an angel with the shepherds and the star over the inn. Move Mary, Joseph, and the innkeeper family into the stable. Place the wise men where they can see, "The Star in the East." (Refer to Appendix A, page 89.)

DECEMBER 25

Addition: BABY JESUS
Baby Jesus is added after the children have gone to bed to be seen by them on Christmas morning.
Activity: Bake Jesus a birthday cake.
Bake a birthday cake using a family recipe, boxed mix or use a pre-made cake. (Refer to Appendix B, page 91.)

Epilogue

It is a long journey from the first day of Advent to Epiphany. (See Appendix A, page 89.) I hope your family enjoyed the trip. Perhaps as you read, "The Children's Nativity," your family will discover a new vision of God's greatest gift – His son, Jesus Christ, and His love for all of you and your family.

May the blessing of peace be with you and your family.

Marti McCartney

Appendix A

Epiphany

Our nativity scene remains up for our enjoyment until January 6, which is called Twelfth Day, Wise Men Day or Epiphany. It is sometimes celebrated as the time the wise men visited the infant Jesus. Some families exchange a small gift today like candy, nuts or fruit.

According to scripture Mary and Jesus were in a house when the Wise Men arrived, therefore it is believed that the Wise men did not reach Bethlehem on the night of his birth.

Matthew 2.9-11

When they [the Wise Men] had heard the king [Herod] they went on their way; and lo, the star, which they had seen in the East went before them, till it came to rest over the place where the child was. When they saw the star, they rejoiced exceedingly with great joy; and going into the house they saw the child with Mary his mother, and they fell down and worshiped him.

Appendix B

Date Cake Recipe

This Date Cake is my favorite cake. My mother made it for me when I was a little girl. I started making it as the birthday cake for Jesus, when my children were little. It is a very moist, rich cake made with nutritious dates and nuts like Joseph and Mary might have eaten on their journey.

Mix together and set aside to soak
1 Cup hot water
8 oz diced dates

Cream together and set aside
½ cup butter
1 Cup sugar
1 teaspoon vanilla
2 eggs

Sift together and set aside
1 ¾ Cup flour
1 teaspoon soda

Stir together and mix well
Date mixture
Butter mixture
Flour mixture

Pour into greased and floured 9 x 12 cake pan.
Sprinkle on top one package chocolate chips and ¾ cup chopped nuts.
Bake 350 degrees for 30 minutes.
A great cake recipe to bake ahead.

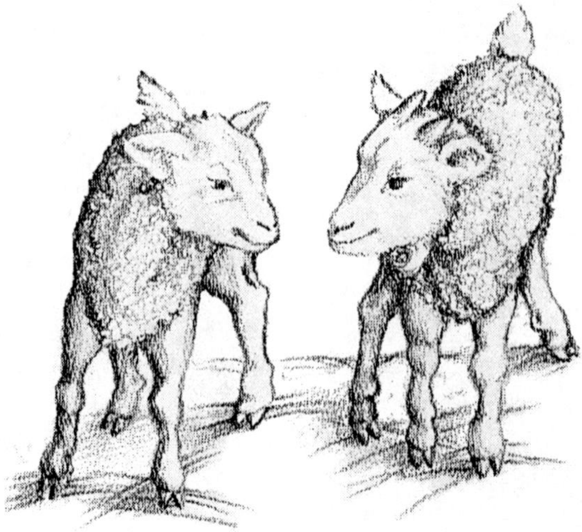

Appendix C

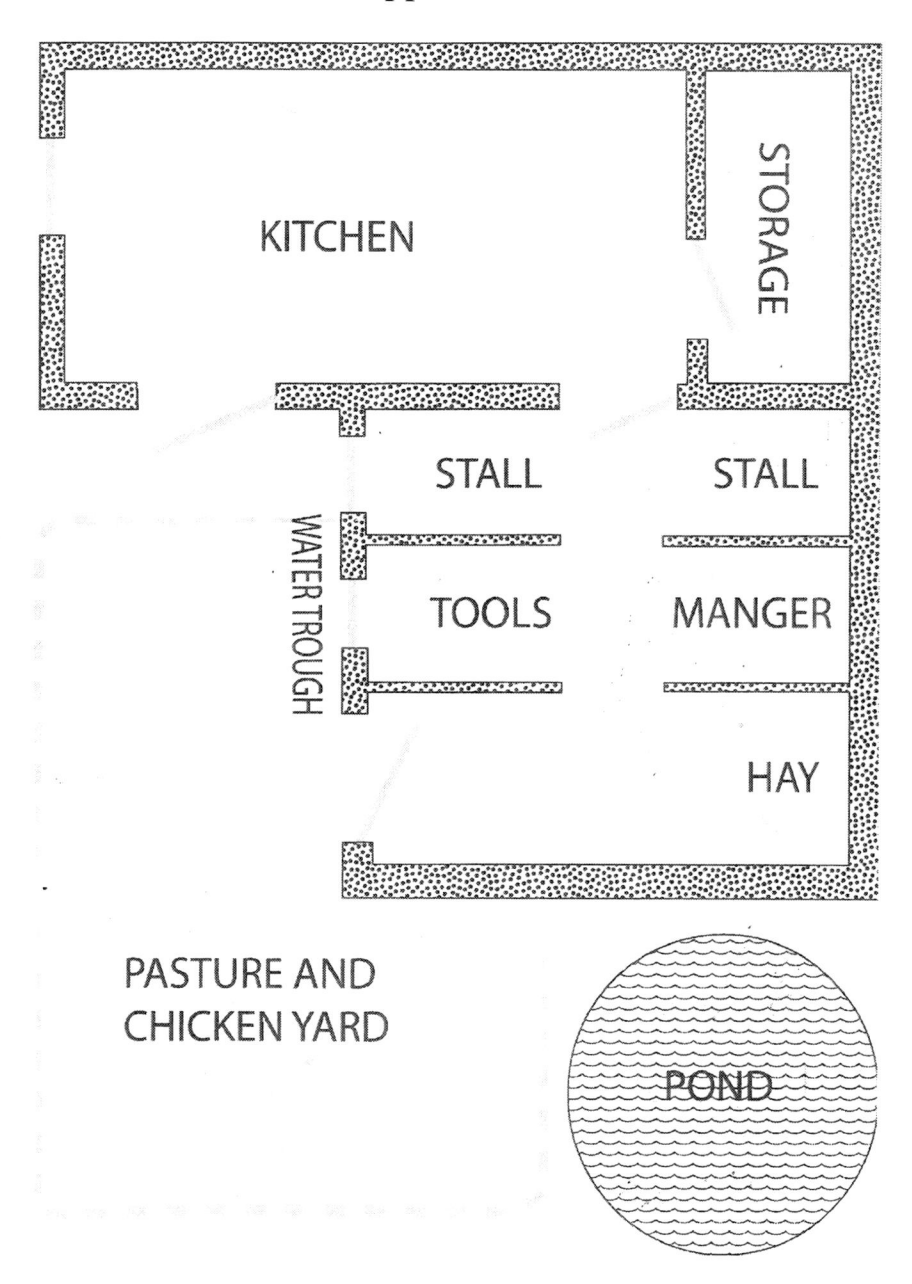

```
                    STORAGE

    KITCHEN


            STALL         STALL
  WATER
  TROUGH
            TOOLS        MANGER


                          HAY


  PASTURE AND
  CHICKEN YARD        POND
```

Marti McCartney

Marti McCartney is a third generation Kansan who lives in Haysville. She homeschooled her children, who are now in college.

Currently, Mrs. McCartney volunteers as a Living History Reenactor at Old Cowtown Museum in Wichita - as well as - the Kansas National Historic Sites of Ft. Scott and Ft. Larned. Her Victorian Presentations can be seen and heard through out the state at organizational meetings, church groups, private homes, museums, festivals, and historic events.

This unique historian plays an 1870s flute, belongs to the Entré Nous Club Victorian Dancers at Old Cowtown Museum and was featured in the publication, "Active Aging." She is an award-winning seamstress and independent scholar for 1800s reproduction garments. Corsetry and underpinning workshops are her specialty.

Alphabetical index

Baby Jesus - December 25
Blanket – December 13
Bread - December 10
Dirt - November 28
Dog - December 9
Donkey - December 23
Doves - December 21
Eggs - December 16
Flies - December 12
Goat - December 11
Grain - December 6
Joseph - December 1
Lamb - December 20
Light - December 3
Mary - December 2
Mousetrap - December 8
Owl - December 22
Oxen - December 7
Rocks - November 29
Rope - December 17
Shepherd - December 19
Straw - December 5
Swaddling Clothes - December 24
Tools - December 14
Water - December 4
Wheel - December 18
Winnowing fork - December 15
Wood - November 30

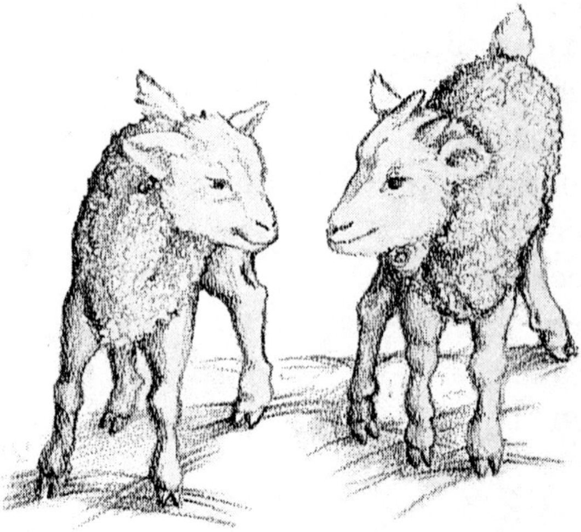

About the Illustrator

Martha Brohammer hails from North East Kansas. She was raised on a farm near Baldwin City, Kansas. She earned her Bachelor's degree in Art Education from the University of Kansas in Lawrence and her Master's degree in Teaching from Friends University in Wichita Kansas. A middle child in a large family of girls, she devoted a large part of her childhood to reading, making art and dreaming about being a teacher and an illustrator. Throughout her teaching career she has taught both Art and Spanish.

Illustrating this book has been a good fit for Ms. Brohammer in three ways. First, the subject of the book, Christmas, is her favorite holiday. And, since she was raised in a largely German community, Christmas is the most important of religious holidays. Second, her childhood on the farm afforded her many opportunities to see, observe, and study different animals -- all of which are included in the illustrations right down to the rats and mice that lived in the barns and other outbuildings. Finally, the genre of the book fits particularly well since it is a book intended to be used for instruction and enrichment. In all, the melding of Ms. Brohammer's own faith and her love of nature permits her illustrations to bring the Christmas story alive.

To order additional copies
or send a comment
please contact:

mccartneymike@sbcglobal.net

CPSIA information can be obtained at www.ICGtesting.com
Printed in the USA
244745LV00002B/3/P